The Kids' Career Library™

A Day in the Life of a
Coach

Dec. 2001

D1745327

Mary Bowman-Kruhm
and Claudine G. Wirths

The Rosen Publishing Group's
PowerKids Press™
New York

Published in 1997 by The Rosen Publishing Group, Inc.
29 East 21st Street, New York, NY 10010

First Edition

Book Design: Erin McKenna

Photo Illustrations: All photo illustrations by Kelly Hahn.

Bowman-Kruhm, Mary.
    A day in the life of a coach / by Mary Bowman-Kruhm and Claudine G. Wirths.
        p.   cm. — (The kids' career library)
    Includes index.
    Summary: Describes some of the activities involved in Coach Jackson's work as an elementary school gym teacher and a high school football coach.
    ISBN 0-8239-5097-2 (lib. bdg.)
    1. Coaches (Athletics)—Juvenile literature. 2. Coaching (Athletics)—Juvenile literature. 3. Football coaches—Juvenile literature. [1. Football coaches. 2. Occupations.] I. Wirths, Claudine G. II. Title. III. Series.
GV711.B69 1996
796'.07'7—dc20
                                                              96-48943
                                                                   CIP
                                                                    AC

Manufactured in the United States of America

Contents

Coach Jackson

Hillcrest **Elementary** (el-uh-MEN-teh-ree) School is empty when Coach Dave Jackson arrives early to start his day as a gym teacher. But students and teachers soon fill the halls. Coach Jackson talks to some of the students while they eat breakfast. The students like to hear about how he studied very hard to become a gym teacher and coach. Next he gets out the **equipment** (ee-KWIP-ment), such as mats and balls, that his classes will need. Then the school day starts and students come to the gym for gym class.

◄ Before class, Coach Jackson finds the equipment he will use.

5

Gym Class

During the first part of class, students work on **fitness** (FIT-ness). They shake their arms. They hop. They jump. Coach Jackson tells them, "Move fast! To be fit and healthy, you have to move fast and get your heart pumping!"

During the last part of class, the students play a game. Some days they play inside. Some days they go outside. Coach Jackson helps them learn how to play the game.

At the beginning of class, Coach Jackson's students work on fitness. ▶

Getting Ready for Practice

After the school day is over, Coach Jackson goes to the high school. During the fall he is the head coach for the football team.

When he arrives, Coach Jackson and one of the **assistant** (uh-SIS-tent) coaches talk about what the team will do during **practice** (PRAK-tis). Next, Coach Jackson watches as some of the players get out the equipment they will need. The players know what to do. Coach Jackson watches to make sure they do a good job.

◀ Coach Jackson talks with one of the assistant coaches about that day's practice.

Practice Begins

While the team warms up, Coach Jackson and the assistant coaches guide the players and build **team spirit** (TEEM SPEER-it).

Time for a **drill** (DRILL)! The team breaks into groups to practice on the field. When the assistant coach blows his **whistle** (WIS-uhl), the players move to a new group. After the drill and a drink of water, Coach Jackson begins to work with the **defensive line** (dee-FEN-siv LYN).

On the field, Coach Jackson works with players on the drills. ▶

Coach and Teacher

First, Coach Jackson works with each player in the defensive line. Next he works with the whole defensive line on **group skills** (GROOP SKILZ). These skills are called "stunts." Coach Jackson has to teach the players lots of stunts so that other teams can't guess what their next move will be. The players practice their stunts. They work hard. Coach Jackson also works hard helping the players to do their best. As a football coach, he is a teacher of the game of football.

◀ Coach Jackson and the players work together on the team's stunts.

Go, Team!

Time for another water break! Now the players are ready to practice together as a full team. The coaches watch as the players try to do everything the coaches have taught them. Coach Jackson cheers for the players and calls out **encouragement** (en-KUR-ej-ment). When the players make mistakes, he calls out helpful ways to fix them.

Coach Jackson helps the players by calling out encouragement. ▶

Game Day

Coach Jackson likes Fridays the best. Friday night is game night. The games are fun and exciting. But they are also a lot of hard work. Coach Jackson must get out the equipment and **supplies** (suh-PLYS) that the team will use. First-aid supplies, cups, and ice are some of the things they will need. While the players put on their uniforms, the coach talks to them about the different plays. He also gets them excited to play the game! The team gives a cheer and runs onto the field.

◀ Coach Jackson gets out the equipment before every game.

During the Game

During the game, Coach Jackson walks up and down the **sidelines** (SYD-lynz). He calls out different plays for the team to use. An assistant coach watches from above the field in the **bleachers** (BLEE-cherz). This coach sees things on the field that Coach Jackson can't see on the ground. Coach Jackson listens on his **headset** (HED-set) to what this coach tells him. Then he passes on what he has learned to the players.

The players listen to what Coach Jackson has learned from the assistant coach. ▶

After the Game

No matter who wins, the coaches and players shake hands with the other team. "Good game," they say. While the players get ready to go home, Coach Jackson is busy. He makes sure all of the equipment is put away. Then the coaches talk to the team about the game. They also check to see if anyone has been hurt. After the players leave, the coaches stay to plan for the next game.

◀ The players listen as Coach Jackson talks to them about the game.

Back for Practice

The players and coaches meet the day after the game. They watch a tape of the game and talk some more about how the team played. What did they do right? What can they do better next time?

Then Coach Jackson goes home to be with his family. Soon Monday will come and he will start his busy week all over again.

Glossary

assistant (uh-SIS-tent) A helper.

bleacher (BLEE-cher) Raised benches that are used for seats.

defensive line (dee-FEN-siv LYN) Part of a team that tries to keep the other team from making a point.

drill (DRILL) A thing done over and over so it is learned.

elementary (el-uh-MEN-teh-ree) Introductory.

encouragement (en-KUR-ej-ment) Giving someone hope and courage to succeed.

equipment (ee-KWIP-ment) Tools or supplies a person uses to do something.

fitness (FIT-ness) Being healthy and strong.

group skill (GROOP SKIL) Something people do very well together through practice.

headset (HED-set) Something you wear on your head that lets you talk and listen to another person who is also wearing one.

practice (PRAK-tis) Doing something over and over to make it perfect.

sidelines (SYD-lynz) The sides of the playing field.

supplies (suh-PLYS) Things a person needs to do a job.

team spirit (TEEM SPEER-it) Feelings of pride and happiness for the people you play with.

whistle (WIS-uhl) An instrument that makes a high sound when air is blown through it.

23

Index